Economic Crisis Observatory

A Service Economy, Atlantic City

Holly Crawford

Lokke
New York

Photographs by Holly Crawford

www.art-poetry.info

All right reserved.

Copyrighted by Holly Crawford, 2011-2013

ISBN-13: 978-0-9852461-6-7
ISBN-10: 0985246162

Most people in the United States now work in the service sector. What does that mean? It means that the United States in the last hundred years has moved from an agricultural economy to a manufacturing economy to a service economy. The labor force moved off the farm and into manufacturing (making steel, automobiles, radios and televisions) into services. This is what they are and what it means.

Service Sector: Government, Telecommunications, Pharmaceuticals, Healthcare, Waste disposal, Education, Banking, Insurance, Financial services, Legal services, Consulting, Information technology, News media, Gambling, Tourism, Retail sales, Franchising, Real estate.

"High-paying manufacturing jobs are rapidly disappearing, only to be replaced by low-paying, and oftentimes menial, service sector jobs that produce absolutely nothing of value, according to the U.S. Labor Department's 2009 Occupational Employment and Wages report."

"The report found that retail sales, cashiers, general office clerks, food preparation and service workers, and nurses were the occupations with the highest levels of employment in 2009.

In fact, nine of the top 10 jobs in the survey pay such low wages that they put a worker supporting a family of four in near poverty." http://economyincrisis.org/content/service-economy-taking-over-us

"The service sector consists of the "soft" parts of the economy, i.e. activities where people offer their knowledge and time to improve productivity, performance, potential, and sustainability. The basic characteristic of this sector is the production of services instead of end products. Services (also known as "intangible goods") include attention, advice, experience, and discussion."

"The tertiary sector of industry involves the provision of services to other businesses as well as final consumers. Services may involve the transport, distribution and sale of goods from producer to a consumer, as may happen in wholesaling and retailing, or may involve the provision of a service, such as in pest control or entertainment. The goods may be transformed in the process of providing the service, as happens in the restaurant industry. However, the focus is on people interacting with people and serving the customer rather than transforming physical goods"

http://en.wikipedia.org/wiki/Service_sector

Atlantic City is an excellent example of a service economy. All most all the people who work there work in the service sector. Tourists come for entertainment and to gamble in hope going home with more money than they came. It is a city now based in one dominant industry—gaming. Monopoly is a game. This is not. Who wins and who loses? Who controls the resources? The text is from sources that I found on Atlantic City on the net.

The text was originally part of an installation, Economic Crisis Observatory, that was exhibited as part of Capital Offense: The End(s) of Capitalism at the Beacon Arts Building, in Southern California very early 2012. It was curated by Jennifer Gradecki and Renée Fox,

In late 2012, I travelled to Atlantic City to take my own pictures for this book. This was only two weeks before hurricane Sandy. When I was there I thought things change fast. Buildings were no longer there. What I found was many empty lots and the casinos. All photographs are taken with a Sony Cybershot camera, in Atlantic City and Margate, New Jersey which is just south of Atlantic City and has an area called Marven Gardens.–Holly Crawford, New York, January 2013.

Please take a seat, relax.

You're going on a ride.

COLLECT $ **?** .00 AS YOU PASS GO.

Round and round you go

MEDITERRANEAN

"This home is in preforeclosure, which means the homeowner is in default (missed payments). Therefore, there could be an opportunity to strike a great deal with the owner and the bank. Condo built in 1987, 1,102 sq. ft."

http://www.zillow.com/homedetails/Mediterranean-Ave-Atlantic-City-NJ-08401/2122631101_zpid/

COMMUNITY CHEST

BALTIC AVENUE

INCOME TAX

"Casinos paid $17 million in taxes on their gross revenues in December. That money, 8 percent of taxable gross revenue, goes into the Casino Revenue Fund, which pays for programs that benefit qualifying senior citizens and people with disabilities. In addition, the casino industry incurred $3.1 million in reinvestment obligations based on their gross revenues for the month. Casinos are required to reinvest 1.25 percent of gross revenues in projects approved by the Casino Reinvestment Development Authority. NJ Department of Law and Public Safety / Office of the Attorney General: Divisions -- Alcoholic Beverage Control " Civil Rights " Consumer Affairs " Criminal Justice "Gaming Enforcement " Highway Traffic Safety " Law " State Police For the year, casinos won $3.3 billion which is down 6.9 percent from 2010. Win from slot machines was down 5.4 percent and win from table games was down 10.4 percent from the prior year. Win reflects the net amount of money won by casinos. It is not profit".

http://www.nj.gov/oag/ge/docs/Financials/PressRel2011/December2011PressRelease.pdf

Transportation I

"The percentages in households with no cars are discretely higher for those residing in poverty. Averaging across all central cities, nearly 47 percent of the central city poor reside in households without a single automobile (with little difference between the elderly and non-elderly). This figure exceeds by far the percent without a car among the poor nationwide.

African-Americans have the lowest car-ownership rates of all racial/ethnic groups. In particular, 19 percent of blacks reside in households without a single car, compared to 4.6 percent of whites, 13.7 percent of Hispanics, and 9.6 percent of those falling into the other category. These racial disparities are particularly large among the poor, suggesting an interaction effect between race and poverty on the likelihood of owning a car."

http://socrates.berkeley.edu/~raphael/BerubeDeakenRaphael.pdf

Vacant Lot for Sale

South Inlet - Casino Zone across from the Revel Casino development. One Block to the Beach and Boardwalk, Corner Lot at Oriental and Vermont.

$199,900

http://www.southjerseyshorehome.com/property/231-oriental-ave-atlantic-city-nj-08401/

Chance

"Atlantic City casinos paid $295.3 million in gaming taxes in 2009, and another $49.3 million to the Casino Reinvestment Development Authority, according to the New Jersey Casino Control Commission.

While Pennsylvania has just nine casinos operating, it has a 55 percent tax rate on slot machine gambling. New Jersey and Nevada place an 8 percent tax on their casinos for both slot-machine and table-game wins combined. New Jersey casinos also pay 1.25 percent of their revenues to the CRDA.

Also, a lower tax rate means Atlantic City's casinos can offer better odds for players, give out more complementary items such as free rooms and meals and bring in first-rate entertainers, Diamond said."

http://www.pressofatlanticcity.com/news/breaking/article_97356818-98cf-11df-8150-001cc4c03286.htmlPosted: Monday, July 26, 2010 12:04 pm | *Updated: 12:35 am, Tue Jul 27, 2010*

VERMONT AVE

Rent: $4,000 a month

"Your palace awaits! This Grand Victorian boasts 5 bedrooms, 3.5 baths. Beautiful hardwood floors, Craftsmen woodwork trim throughout. Imported crystal chandeliers enhance every room! Marble floors and granite countertops in a spacious eat in kitchen."

http://www.zillow.com/homedetails/34-N-Vermont-Ave-Atlantic-City-NJ-08401/52664973_zpid/

CONNECTICUT AVE

Multi-family housing, 4 units in building.

31 S Connecticut Ave Huge possiblities, location close to new Casino. Being sold strictly "As Is". Buyer responsible for all Certs and CO.

http://www.trulia.com/property/3014745986-31-S-Connecticut-Ave-Atlantic-City-NJ-08401

JAIL

CHANCES OF BECOMING A VICTIM

Atlantic City   **1 in 61**

New Jersey   **1 in 308**

Rate Per 1,000	murder	rape	robbery
Atlantic City	0.30	0.91	7.11
United States	0.05	0.29	1.45

http://www.neighborhoodscout.com/nj/atlantic-city/crime/

ST. CHARLES PLACE

Weekly Rate, summer 2011

$2675 - $3750

"There are gorgeous ocean views from the bedrooms, porch and deck. The furnishings are French traditional with antique accents. The split level design and great room make it perfectly comfortable for family. Sleeps 8."

http://www.zillow.com/homedetails/34-N-Vermont-Ave-Atlantic-City-NJ08401/52664973_zpid/

Where is St. Charles Place?

ELECTRIC COMPANY

"Between 1998 and 2001, Trump Taj Mahal Casino Resort was overbilled nearly $1.5 million in utility taxes, Trump Marina Hotel Casino about $670,000 and Trump Plaza Hotel and Casino almost $540,000."

"The dispute was related to a contract between Trump and Atlantic City Electric that exempted the casinos from a state utility tax enacted by the Legislature in 1998."

STATES AVE

From major sales accounts to fast-food workers, sales and service employees are often the backbone of the local economy. Analysis identifies this neighborhood has a higher percentage of sales and service workers than 99.9% of all American neighborhoods.

Pacific Ave / States Ave neighborhood in Atlantic City are low income, making it among the lowest income neighborhoods in America. This neighborhood has an income lower than 95.4% of U.S. neighborhoods. With 23.6% of the children here below the federal poverty line, this neighborhood has a higher rate of childhood poverty than 83.7% of U.S. neighborhoods.

http://www.neighborhoodscout.com/nj/atlantic-city/pacific-states/#desc

States Avenue is now parking lots and empty lots. Where did they go? Some new housing looks like it was built, but many people were coming and going from the bus station. Those were the people with jobs. Many people were at the Rescue Mission.

VIRGINIA AVE

Trump Taj Mahal

"Il Mulino New York- Atlantic City brings the highest quality ingredients and technique, authentic preparations of the Abruzzi region of Italy, and flawless service to Atlantic City's Trump Taj Mahal. A destination for high rollers and lovers of fine cuisine alike, the restaurant offers a luxurious dining experience unparalleled even in this opulent city."

"The food was fantastic. Would have been good to have a better understanding of how the dinner would go. First you are seated and go through the complimentary starters (which they didn't let us know were complimentary or how the schedule would be until we complained about not getting a menu). We made it out of there at $175 (pre-tip) for 4, including a bottle of wine. We were offered coffee/latte at the end but didn't know they too were complimentary until the waiter was walking away. They did give us a shot of refined processed grape skins (very strong) which was also included. Overall very good, but would have liked to have a waiter explain everything promptly at the start so you aren't wondering how much your bill is going to be at the end."

http://www.opentable.com/il-mulino-new-york-atlantic-city

TRANSPORTATION II

The South Jersey Transportation Authority operates shuttle buses and vans that bridge the gap between employers and qualified employees. The SJTA can help employers fill job openings from a pool of qualified workers and also help transport them to work.

- Provide service to worksites in Burlington, Camden and Gloucester counties (See Pureland Shuttle under Gloucester County).
- Operate seven days a week, serving most shifts.
- Serve employment sites throughout South Jersey and qualified tri-county residents.
- Offer convenient pick-up and drop-off locations for employees that connect to other public transportation services, including:
    - The Rand Transportation Center
    - PATCO Stations
    - Atlantic City Rail Line Stations
    - River LINE Stations
- Provide direct service to employment sites, transporting employees from near their homes during late night hours.
- Offer free service to employers and employees.

http://www.sjta.com/acexpressway/employers.asp

The Irish Pub

ST. JAMES PLACE

"If you're looking to experience a taste of the old Atlantic City, as depicted in the popular HBO series "Boardwalk Empire," look no further than The Irish Pub. In fact, The Irish Pub, at one time, was a speakeasy, back in the days of prohibition. The history of the Irish Pub dates back to the 19th century. It has survived hurricanes, prohibition, two world wars, high tides and low tides. It has fed the famous and infamous and if you sit at the front table it is said eventually everybody in the world would pass by you. Joe DiMaggio stayed at the Inn for many years. Being situated on St. James Place & the Boardwalk, it has been identified with the game of Monopoly and the red hotels used in the game are based on the architecture of the Irish Pub."

COMMUNITY CHEST

Social Services

1301 Bacharach Blvd, Room 130
Atlantic City, NJ 08401

The Social Services Division primarily reaches out to seniors (60 years and over) and will assist with Home Energy Assistance programs, Cooling Assistance programs, Lifeline Applications, Transportation, Meals on Wheels and Food Stamps. Additionally, they have information and referrals to a wide variety of agencies based on the needs of the client.

Director Currently Vacant

http://www.cityofatlanticcity.org/divdetails.aspx?dva=ssd

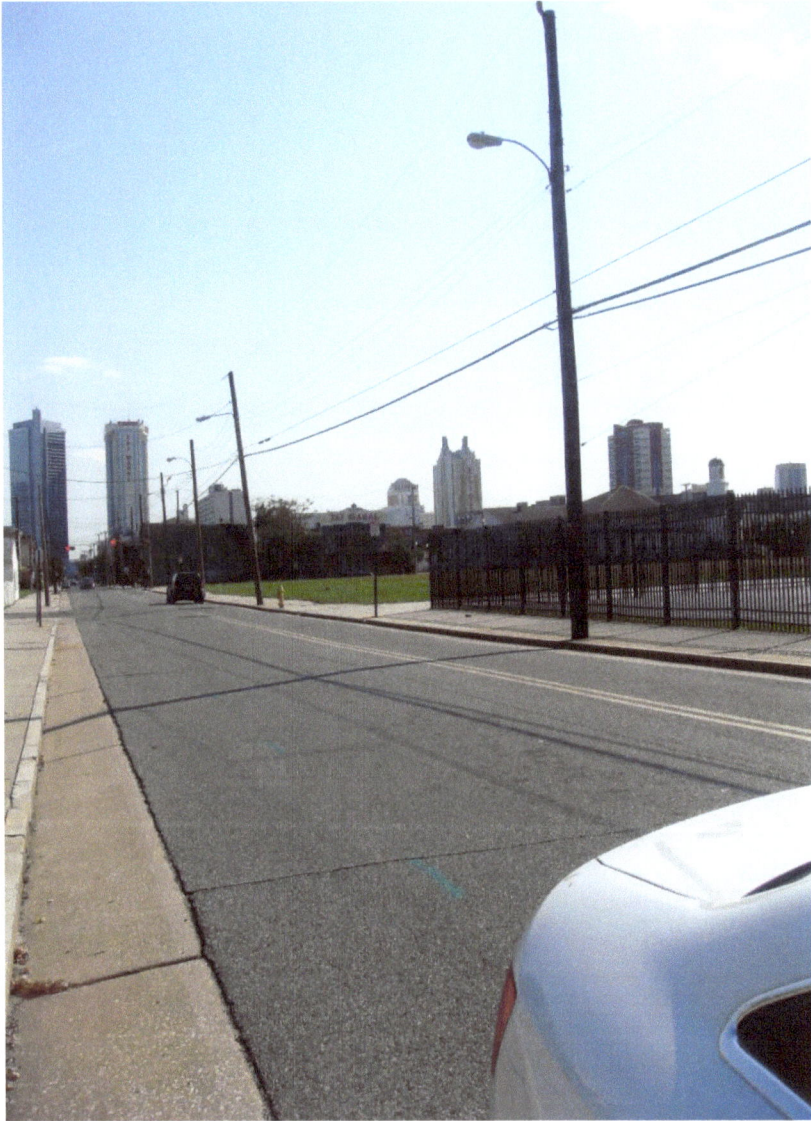

TENNESSEE AVE

$93.03 a night king smoking

Super 8 Atlantic City, close to Ripley's Believe It or Not Odditorium, Steel Pier, and Central Pier. Nearby points of interest also include Atlantic City Public Library and Atlantic City Hall.

The motel serves a complimentary continental breakfast. Guest parking is complimentary.

68 air-conditioned guestrooms feature coffee/tea makers. Wireless Internet access is available. Premium cable television is provided.

http://www.hotelplanner.com/Hotels/91555/Reservations-Super-8-Atlantic-City-Atlantic-City-175-South-Tennessee-Ave-08401

NEW YORK AVE

Parking on New York Ave.

Open 24 hours.

Daily Rates:

UP TO 2 HOURS -------- $ 3

After the 3rd hour -------- $ 4

After the 4th hour -------- $ 5

After the 5th hour ------- $ 6

Maximum for 24 hours - $ 7

http://www.sjta.com/sjta/parking.asp

EXIT ONLY

19
SOUTH
NEW YORK A

CAUT
VEHIC
EXIT

FREE PARKING

"Welcome to Atlantic City, New Jersey's Playground! Investors Delight or Second home that requires some sweat-equity! The possibilities are endless! This Property is Fixer-up. Use Caution - Weak flooring upon entry and through-out. As-Is-Sale "

http://www.trulia.com/property/3073229113-659-N-New-York-Ave-Atlantic-City-NJ-08401

KENTUCKY AVE

"A fledgling development group wants to restore Kentucky Avenue into an entertainment district that would offer lower-cost, smaller venue options than casinos typically provide."

http://www.pressofatlanticcity.com/news/breaking/development-group-wants-to-restore-atlantic-city-s-kentucky-avenue/article_b40f8a2e-49da-11e0-8d5c-001cc4c002e0.html

"The popular nightclubs near KY and the Curb - Club Harlem, Little Belmont, Paradise Club, Wonder Garden and Wonder Bar - attracted such stars as Louis Armstrong, Ella Fitzgerald, Count Basie, Ethel Waters, Nat King Cole, Lena Horne, Duke Ellington, Billie Holiday, Cab Calloway, Frank Sinatra, and Dinah Washington. Crowds from all walks of life filled the streets and clubs, for the programs on Saturday nights and the "breakfast shows" on Sunday mornings. It was difficult to even walk down Kentucky Avenue at times because of all the people waiting to get into the various clubs and the restaurants. By the late 1960s the area was changing. City casino, opened in 1978."

http://www.atlanticcityexperience.org/index.php?option=com_content&view=article&id=28&Itemid=27

CHANCE

Text on electric box surrounded by empty lots reads "Please let us shine." It is on the corner of Baltic Ave, but there is no street sign.

INDIANA AVE

"ACT NOW! TURNKEY OPERATION- RENOVATED 4UNIT MULTIPLEX- 100% OCCUPANCY- GREAT CONDITION- RENT: THREE, 4BR UNITS @$1350.00 PER MOS- 1 EFFICIENCY @$675.00 PER MOS- ANNUAL INCOME $56,700.00- TAXES $477.00 PER MOS- SEPERATE METERS- TENANTS PAY ALL UTILITIES- WHAT AN AMAZING POSITIVE CASH FLOW & GREAT BUY."

"Formerly a single-Family Home located at 607 North Indiana Avenue, sold for $230,000 on Mar 28, 2011. It is approximately 4,139 sq. ft. The house was built in 1918. Sold for, $100,000 on Aug 5, 2008, and $314,500 on Sep 29, 2003."

http://www.zillow.com/homedetails/607-N-Indiana-Ave-Atlantic-City-NJ-08401/52669166_zpid/

ILLINOIS AVE

"This architectural treasure, originally completed in 1904, was a gift to the residents of Atlantic City by steel magnate and philanthropist Andrew Carnegie."

http://intraweb.stockton.edu/eyos/page.cfm?siteID=257&pageID=1

"The Carnegie Library is located at the corner of Pacific and Dr. Martin Luther King, Jr. Blvd. (formerly Illinois Avenue). The Carnegie Center of Stockton College of NJ now hosts undergraduate and graduate courses continuing professional education programming, and special events relevant to the needs of Atlantic City and its surrounding region. Stockton College public college with an undergraduate enrollment of 78% white students and 8% black. The population of Atlantic City is   44% black, 26% white 24% latino …."

http://intraweb.stockton.edu/eyos/aboutstockton/content/docs/College_Portrait-Richard_Stockton_College_of_New_Jersey.pdf
http://atlanticcity.areaconnect.com/statistics.htm

It is now the center for the study of gaming.

ALANTIC AVENUE

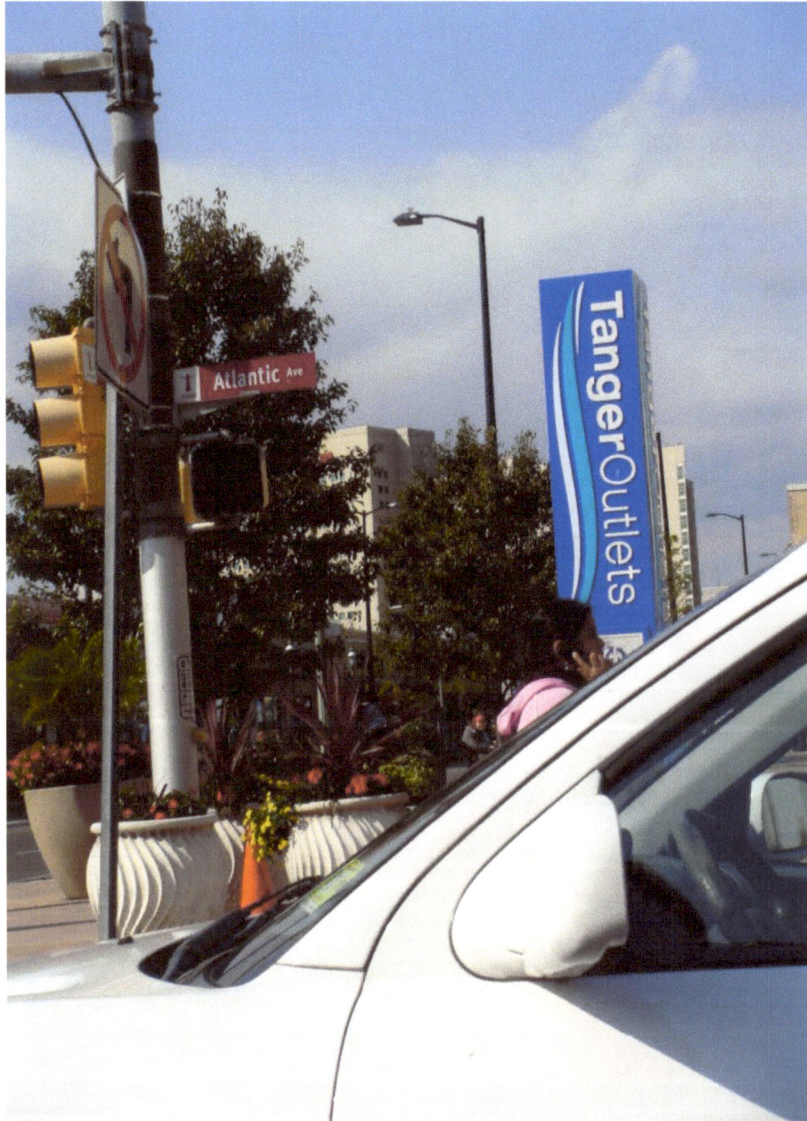

New outlets shopping at Atlantic and Baltic

VENTOR AVENUE

WATER WORKS

"WILL BE A 5 % INCREASE IN RATES FOR WATER SERVICE IN 2012"

"Over the last several years, the Atlantic City Municipal Utilities Authority (MUA) has seen its expenses rise, however, water demand (and the resulting revenue), since 2006, has shown a steady and continual decline. The MUA attributes the decline to two (2) primary factors. The first is the removal of hotels and housing in Atlantic City through demolition. Projects such as the Pinnacle that took the Sand's Casino Hotel out of service and demolished it, as well as several other hotels in the area had a significant detrimental effect on the MUA's revenues. The next most significant factor in the MUA's revenue decline is water conserving devices. Water conversation is always promoted in order to minimize the wasteful use of resources. Since 1992, the MUA has seen the average gallons per capita per day in Atlantic City for residential customers drop from 97 to 73, almost a twenty-five (25%) percent reduction. This trend continued through 2011. Last year's rate increase combined with significant reductions in expenses due to changing energy providers and changing the after-hours staffing allowed the MUA to stabilize its finances.

The MUA's proposed 5 % increase will be applied as a 6 % increase in base charges and an increase of 3.5 % in excess charges, for all users in all categories in Atlantic City. The average residential single family property in Atlantic City currently pays approximately $199.41 per year for water. The MUA is currently projecting that, with this rate increase, the average consumer will pay $210.75 per year. This is an $11.34 per year increase."

MARVIN GARDEN

Marven Gardens area of Margate on the beach looking north to Atlantic City.

Marven Gardens (Margate, NJ) "Is located 3 miles south of Atlantic City in the town of Margate. For many years, houses in the neighborhood fell into disrepair. During the housing boom of the 2000s, though, many houses changed ownership and have been returned to their former beauty. In the past ten years, a group of residents got grant money from the City of Margate to restore the numerous landscaped islands throughout the development by planting hundreds of rose bushes, junipers and hydrangeas. Marven Gardens is one of the most expensive streets in Margate. It has some of the highest price per square foot rates in New Jersey."

http://en.wikipedia.org/wiki/Marven_Gardens

Margate's Marven Gardens

PACIFIC AVENUE

The Carnegie Library at the corners of Pacific and Illinois. The motto carved over what was the main door. It is now a center to study gaming that is part of Stockton University. It is no longer open to all.

NORTH CAROLINE AVENUE

PENNYSLVANNIA AVENUE

Description

Whiskey Grill Restaurant & Bar w/ all F, F & E. Also 9
Apartments: 2-studios,4-1 BR, 3-2 BR. Located in the
CBD and the Tourist Zone and the across from
The Trump Executive Offices.

$599,000
Vacant/Owner-User

Last Verified 12/27/2011 Listing ID 17241143

TRANSPORTATION

CHANCE

PARK PLACE

Experience Total Romance starting at $148

Escape to our seaside getaway and experience passion like never before. Can't you just imagine strolling the beach with your lover as you watch the winter waves roll in? Then warming up with a gourmet dinner for two and all the thrills Bally's has to offer before cozying up in your sumptuous guest room. The next morning, you'll awaken to a romantic breakfast in bed. A late checkout means you have time to indulge in the fantasy even longer.

Your package includes:

- Overnight accommodations for one (1) night at Bally's

- Four Course Gourmet Dinner for Two at Arturo's or The Reserve (from Pre-Fixe $39 Fine Dining Menu or $78 credit)

- Breakfast in bed for two

- Access for 2 to the health spa

- Late check out at 1 p.m.

https://www.totalrewards.com/hotel-reservations/main/?propCode=BAC&view=packagesearch#

LUXURY TAX

Description
The Atlantic City Luxury Sales Tax applies to the receipts from specified retail sales within Atlantic City, including sales of alcoholic beverages for on-premises consumption; cover, minimum, or entertainment charges; room rental in hotels, inns, rooming, or boarding houses; hiring of rolling chairs, beach chairs, and cabanas; and tickets of admission within Atlantic City.

Rate
The rate of tax is 3% on sales of alcoholic beverages sold by the drink and 9% on other taxable sales. The maximum combined Atlantic City rate and New Jersey State sales tax rate (excluding the State occupancy fee) may not exceed 13% effective July 15, 2006. The State sales tax rate is reduced to the extent that the city rate exceeds 7%, and the maximum combined Atlantic City rate and New Jersey rate may not exceed 13%. Formerly, the maximum combined Atlantic City rate and the New Jersey sales tax rate could not exceed 12%.

http://www.state.nj.us/treasury/taxation/acluxury_over.shtml

BROADWALK

"In the morning on 09/03/11 I woke up from a burning sensation in my right ring finger. It was swollen and itchy. As I looked up my right arm I discovered 4 more red/swollen bumps. I thought of mosquito bites, although I haven't been outside since we arrived to the hotel, and consider a 36th floor with no open windows made me suspect bed bugs. Me and my son started to examine the bed, mattresses and wooden head-boards, but find nothing. We called front desk, but were told that we need to come to speak to supervisor. I still could not believe in possibility of bed bugs in such upscale hotel. How wrong I was! Next night I could not sleep well, and at some point felt something was biting on my upper right arm. I turned on light and see something small scattering under the pillow. I managed to catch it and there it was - a small bed bug. As I lifted a blanket - another one try to hide. Over all I sustained about 20 bites on my right arm and 6 on my left leg. My son had 6 bites on his arms, and some on his leg. The way hotel handled it - is another story."-- http://bedbugregistry.com/

Economic Crisis Observatory, Beacon Arts Building, mixed media participation installation, size variable, 20012.

www.ingramcontent.com/pod-product-compliance
Lightning Source LLC
Chambersburg PA
CBHW052053190326
41519CB00002BA/208